W9-CJL-412

ELEPHANT

by CAROLINE ARNOLD
Photographs by RICHARD HEWETT

MORROW JUNIOR BOOKS · NEW YORK

PHOTO CREDITS
Permission to use the following photograph is gratefully acknowledged: Caroline Arnold, page 19.

The text type is 14-point Galliard.
1 2 3 4 5 6 7 8 9 10
Library of Congress Cataloging-in-Publication Data Arnold, Caroline. Elephant / Caroline Arnold ; photographs by Richard Hewett.   p. cm.
Summary: Provides information about the physical characteristics and habits of African and Asian elephants in the wild and in captivity.   ISBN 0-688-11344-3 (trade).—ISBN 0-688-11345-1 (library)   1. Elephants—Juvenile literature. [1. Elephants.] I. Hewett, Richard, ill. II. Title.   QL737.P98A76 1993 599.6'1—dc20 92-31094 CIP AC

ACKNOWLEDGMENTS

We are extremely grateful to Marine World Africa USA in Vallejo, California, for their cooperation on this project and for allowing us to get to know and photograph their elephants. In particular, we want to thank Jim Bonde, public relations; Darryl Bush, photographer; and everyone on the Elephant Encounter training staff, especially David Blasko, manager; Pat Flora, supervisor; and Patrick Chapple, trainer (pictured at right). The elephants at Marine World Africa USA include seven Asians—Mardji (age forty-two), Bandula (twenty-four), Roman (eight), Judy (twenty-seven), Taj (fifty-two), Tina (thirty-five), and Ginny (fifty-three)—and four Africans—Tika (age fourteen), Tava (fourteen), Misha (eleven), and Mailika (four).

We also want to thank Cecile Fisher and Tom Lewis at the Natural History Museum of Los Angeles County for their assistance regarding elephant tusks and teeth. And, as always, we thank our editor, Andrea Curley, for her continued enthusiastic support.

F lanked on either side by an adult elephant, four-year-old Mailika ambles slowly across the sloping field. The rising sun warms her leathery skin, and through her hollow trunk she can smell the fresh morning air.

As they walk, the elephants trample the newly green grass with their feet, occasionally stopping to pluck tender clumps to eat. With huge appetites to match their giant bodies, elephants are the largest living land animals.

5

Mailika is the youngest of eleven elephants that live at Marine World Africa USA, a wild animal park in northern California. Mailika's name means "angel" in Swahili, one of the languages spoken in Zimbabwe, East Africa, where she was born. Mailika is nearly twice as big as she was at birth; but compared with the older elephants, she is still quite small. By the time she is fully grown she will weigh 5 tons (4.5 metric tons) or more.

Along with the great apes and dolphins, elephants are among the most intelligent of all animals. They learn quickly, have good memories, and can be trained to do a wide variety of tasks. At the wildlife park, trainers work with the elephants each day to practice old skills and learn new ones. These sessions provide the elephants with both physical and mental exercise. Most of the elephants' "tricks" are adaptations of their natural be-

haviors. Walking, running, lifting, pushing, and manipulating objects with their trunks are actions that wild elephants do every day. A trained elephant is directed to do these behaviors on command. Although the park elephants are tame, the trainers are always careful when working with them because, like all wild animals, elephants can be dangerous. The trainers and the elephants know one another well and develop good relationships that are based on mutual trust, respect, and affection.

A morning walk is part of the elephants' usual daily routine. They line up single file and each elephant is directed to grasp the tail of the preceding elephant in its trunk. In this formation the elephants are said to be "tailed up." Then they are ready to march through the park so visitors can meet them and learn more about them.

The group of elephants at Marine World Africa USA includes ten females and one male, ranging in age from four to fifty-three. The elephants get along well together and each has its own distinct personality. For instance, one of the oldest elephants, Mardji, enjoys being petted; Judy likes to "borrow" her neighbor's food at feeding time; and fourteen-year-old Tava is noted for her curiosity.

All day long people can see the elephants in a variety of situations. They can watch them do circus tricks, play games with a ball, or demonstrate pulling and lifting techniques. People can also ride an elephant and watch the elephants as they relax in their outdoor enclosure. Mailika seems to enjoy her time performing and, as she circles the ring to pick up small biscuit treats, people have a chance to see her up close.

American mastodon (left); woolly mammoth (center); modern Asian male (right).

Elephants and their relatives belong to a large group of animals called Proboscids, a name that comes from a Greek word referring to their long trunks. Besides elephants, the only Proboscids living today are manatees, hyraxes, and dugongs. However, these animals bear little resemblance to elephants and are so distantly related that some scientists classify them in other groups. One of the earliest Proboscids was a small animal called *Moeritherium* that lived in Egypt 45 million years ago. Its descendants, which lived on every continent except Australia and Antarctica, include more than 350 species. This number has been declining steadily over the last 3 million years. The closest relatives of present-day elephants are the mammoths and mastodons of prehistoric times. These large animals, which were hunted by early humans, died out at the end of the last Ice Age about 10,000 years ago, when changes in the climate and food supply caused the extinction of many large mammals. Today there are only two species of elephants, the African and Asian. In the wild, these, too, are threatened with extinction due to illegal hunting and the loss of their natural habitat.

The African elephant is found across the central portion of Africa south of the Sahara. Most elephants live in grasslands and open woodlands although they can adapt to a wide variety of habitats. A subspecies of the African elephant called the forest elephant lives in the dense forests of the Congo River Basin in the central and western parts of the continent. It is slightly smaller than the elephants of the plains, has thinner, pinkish tusks, and has smaller, slightly rounded ears.

Wild Asian elephants live in the hilly forests of India, Sri Lanka, Southeast Asia, southern China, and the islands of Sumatra and Borneo. In ancient times Asian elephants were also found as far west as present-day Iran, on the island of Java, and throughout much of China. For many centuries, people have used Asian elephants as work animals. Although African elephants can also be trained and are often seen in circuses, they were never widely domesticated in the same way that Asian elephants have been.

Although both species of elephant share many behaviors and characteristics, they differ enough in their appearance that it is easy to tell them apart. African elephants are the larger of the two species. A full-grown African male can stand 13 feet (3.9 meters) tall at the shoulder and weigh more than 7 tons (6.3 metric tons). Asian males are about 9 feet (2.7 meters) tall and weigh about 6 tons (5.4 metric tons). Females of both species are about 18 inches (46.2 centimeters) shorter and weigh 1 to 2 tons (.9 to 1.8 metric tons) less. The group of elephants at Marine World Africa USA is composed of both Africans and Asians.

African elephants also have much larger ears than their Asian relatives. A single ear may weigh up to 110 pounds (50 kilograms). The Asian elephant's smaller ears are better suited to forest life because they are less likely to catch on low-hanging vines and branches.

The profiles of the two species are also quite different. The African elephant usually carries its head high and has a flat, sloping forehead. The Asian elephant carries its head lower and its forehead has two large bumps. The back of the Asian elephant rises slightly in the center to form a hump, while the African elephant's back dips slightly in the middle.

The skin of African elephants tends to be rougher than that of Asian elephants and its trunk is ridged. The tip of an African elephant's trunk has two fingerlike projections, called *processes*, one above the other. The Asian elephant's smooth-skinned trunk has only one process at the top.

Among African elephants, both males and females have long tusks. Those of females, however, are somewhat more slender. With Asian elephants, only males have visible tusks and for that reason are sometimes called "tuskers." Asian females have no tusks at all or only small tusks that do not reach beyond the jaw.

Elephants' tusks originally developed from structures in the mouth that, in other animals, form two of the front teeth. Except for the enamel tip, the tusk is solid ivory. A baby elephant is born with two small tusks. They grow to about 2 inches (5.1 centimeters) in length and then are shed during the youngster's second year. Permanent tusks appear when the elephant is about two years old and continue growing about 1 inch (2.6 centimeters) a year throughout the elephant's life. Only two thirds of the tusk is visible; the rest is attached to the bones of the skull. The tusks of an old animal can be enormous. The heaviest pair of tusks ever measured weighed 440 pounds (200 kilograms). The longest was 11½ feet (3.5 meters) in length.

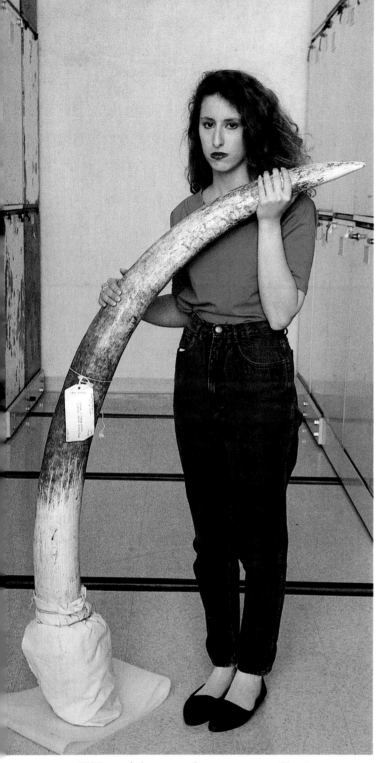

This tusk is part of a museum collection.

Elephants sometimes use their tusks as weapons to defend themselves or when fighting other elephants. More often, though, tusks are used as tools. When wild elephants feed, they use their tusks as giant levers to knock over or uproot trees. Once the tree is felled, the elephant can easily eat the top leaves that had been out of reach before. Tusks are also useful for digging holes to find water or salt underground.

For thousands of years people have used ivory from elephant tusks to make jewelry, sculptures, medicines, and other things. The ruthless killing of these animals for their tusks is one of the reasons the number of elephants has declined so dramatically in recent years. Despite international bans on the sale of ivory, elephants continue to be killed by poachers, people who hunt illegally. In Africa today, fewer than 650,000 elephants remain in the area where twice as many lived just ten years ago. In Asia, there are fewer than 40,000 wild elephants, and about 16,000 more in captivity are used for work.

In the wild, elephants live in family groups, called *herds*, composed of closely related females and their offspring. The adult females take turns watching the youngsters and sometimes even share nursing duties.

Each family herd usually has about twelve animals. Herds sometimes join one another temporarily, occasionally forming huge groups of 100 animals or more. The leader of each small herd is one of the older, more experienced females. It is her responsibility to lead the group to food and water, and to detect danger.

As youngsters grow up, they learn how to survive from the older elephants in the herd. But when poachers kill older elephants for their tusks, younger members of a family herd may be left without adults that can show them how to find the things they need to live.

Like most elephants in captivity, Mailika was born in the wild. She came to Marine World Africa USA when she was two and a half years old, after her mother and the other adults in her herd had been killed by hunters. When Mailika joined the elephant group at the wildlife park, twelve-year-old Tika, one of the African females, developed a close relationship with her and became a kind of substitute mother.

Male elephants are called *bulls,* the females, *cows,* and the youngsters, *calves.* Both males and females reach full growth when they are about twenty-five. A female elephant usually remains with her mother's herd for her whole life. A young male elephant leaves the herd when he is about fifteen years old and for a few years may travel with another young male. An older adult male usually lives alone except when he temporarily joins a herd to mate with a female. He can tell that she is ready to mate by her scent and her behavior.

Bull elephants are capable of mating as early as the age of eleven or twelve, though they rarely get the chance to do so. Most mating is done by older bulls. About once a year a bull elephant goes into a condition known as *musth*. At that time a small gland between each eye and ear swells and produces a dark, oily liquid that oozes down over the face. A bull in musth often becomes aggressive and will fight with other bulls for the right to mate with a female. The bull in musth may win a contest against a stronger bull if the other bull is not in musth. After the bull has mated, he leaves the herd and resumes his solitary life. Musth is rarely seen in zoo or circus elephants because most captive elephants are female.

A cow elephant may reproduce as early as the age of twelve, but usually she has her first calf when she is about sixteen years old. Following a successful mating the female is pregnant for nineteen to twenty-two months. After her long pregnancy, the female elephant produces a single calf. (Twins occur only rarely.) She will not mate again until the calf is about a year and a half old. A cow has a new calf about once every three years and may continue to produce calves up to the age of sixty or more.

When it is time for her calf to be born, the female elephant finds a secluded thicket and then uses her feet to scrape the ground clean and smooth. She gives birth standing up, allowing the baby to drop to the ground. During the birth, one or more adult females from the herd often stand by as guards against danger.

The newborn calf weighs between 180 and 225 pounds (81.8–102.3 kilograms) and stands about 3 feet (.91 meter) high at the shoulder. As with other mammals, a baby elephant's first food is its mother's milk. The mother's two teats are located on the underside of her body just behind the front legs. The baby elephant sucks with its mouth, allowing its tiny trunk to flop to the side so that it is out of the way.

Older African females protect a young calf in a national park in western Uganda.

Perhaps the most unique feature of an elephant is its trunk. An elephant cannot lower its head or mouth to the ground. Instead, it uses its trunk to pick up objects, to bring food and water to its mouth, and sometimes to throw things. The trunk is sensitive to touch and helps the elephant to feel the shape, texture, and temperature of its surroundings. Elephants also touch and caress one another with their trunks in greeting. A young elephant learns how to use its trunk by trial and error, gradually becoming more adept.

The trunk is formed by a combination of the elephant's upper lip and nose, which, over millions of years, became extremely long and specialized. Forty thousand muscles and tendons in the trunk make it strong and flexible. The elephant can wrap its trunk around large objects to pull or lift them, or it can perform a very delicate task such as picking up an object as small as a berry.

20

An elephant has an excellent sense of smell and uses odors detected with its trunk to identify objects and to determine whether something might be good to eat. An elephant breathes through the nostrils at the end of its trunk. In one of the performances at the animal park, an elephant holds a harmonica in its trunk and plays it by breathing in and out.

An excited or angry elephant sometimes raises its trunk and makes a loud, trumpeting noise. Other sounds that elephants make include barks, snorts, screams, roars, growls, thumps, and rumbles. Elephants use sounds to direct one another to food and water, warn one another of danger, coordinate herd movements, and find mates. Some of their noises contain infrasounds, extremely low sounds that are below the range of human hearing. Like thunder, which also contains infrasounds, these low noises travel well over long distances. Elephants can use them to communicate with one another even when they are many miles apart.

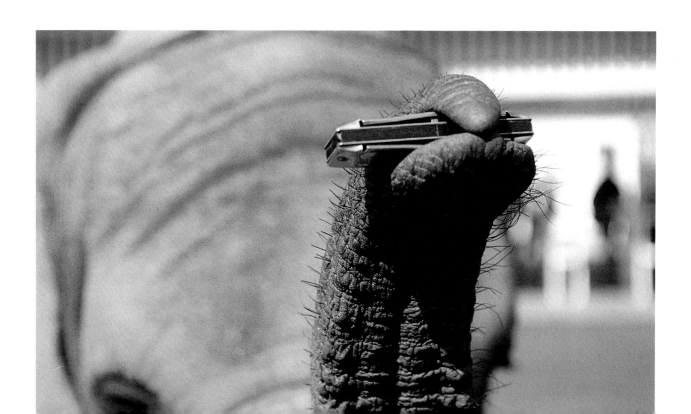

The elephant's tail ends with strands of wiry hairs (left). Long lashes fringe the upper eyelid (right).

Elephants are mammals, and one characteristic of mammals is that they have hair or fur. At birth an elephant calf is covered with short hairs, but these gradually fall out as the animal grows older. On the body of an adult elephant, the hair is so sparse that the skin is mostly bare. The only visible clumps of hair are on the eyelids and eyebrows, and on the end of the tail. The elephant's ropelike tail is about 6 feet (1.83 meters) long and weighs about 40 pounds (18.2 kilograms). The coarse black hairs at its end help make it a good flyswatter.

An elephant's eyelashes can be up to 3 inches (7.7 centimeters) long. They protect the eyes from flying dust or other objects. A thin, semitransparent eyelid called the *nictitating membrane* slides across the eye sideways and provides additional protection. Compared with humans, elephants do not see especially well, and, in relation to the rest of the body, the elephant's eyes are quite small.

Tough skin protects the elephant's body. Elephants are sometimes called *pachyderms,* a Greek word meaning "thick skin," and on some parts of the elephant's body the skin is 1 inch (2.6 centimeters) thick. At the joints and in back it is attached rather loosely, giving the elephant its saggy, baggy look. The skin of most elephants is dark gray, although some Asian elephants are marked with pink-and-white blotches. The famous white elephants of Asia are born with little skin pigment in their eyes and between their skin folds. They are sacred in the Buddhist religion.

Despite its thickness, an elephant's skin is easily irritated. Dust and mud baths help to protect the sensitive skin from insects and the hot sun.

The elephant's skin feels like leather.

Elephants live in parts of the world where the weather is often hot. An elephant's ears are important for regulating body temperature, especially where there is little shade. Within the ears are many tiny blood vessels. Air passing over the ears helps to cool the blood, which then travels to other parts of the body and cools them. The temperature of the blood in the ears can be as much as 10 degrees Fahrenheit (5.5 degrees Celsius) different from that in the body.

Another way that elephants keep cool is by going into water, and they may bathe three or more times a day. In shallow water, elephants use their trunks to spray water over their backs. In deep water, they may stay completely submerged except for their trunks, which they use like snorkels for breathing. Elephants are good swimmers and have been known to swim for six hours without resting. At the animal park a pond in their outdoor enclosure allows the elephants to bathe whenever they want. Trainers also hose off the animals regularly to keep them clean and cool.

A fiberglass model of the bones in an elephant's foot (left). (Only three of the five toes can be seen.) A heavy file helps smooth the rough edges of the toenail (right).

The elephant's strong, straight legs resemble sturdy tree trunks and help support the enormous weight of its body. Although elephants cannot jump or leap, they are remarkably surefooted. At the wildlife park, they show their good sense of balance by walking the length of a log like gymnasts on a balance beam. The elephant walks on its toes, which, along with the rest of the bones of the foot, are surrounded by flesh and muscle to form a flat surface. The soft cushions between the toes work like shock absorbers, padding the impact of the elephant's heavy steps as it walks across uneven ground. They also allow the elephant to walk very quietly. Despite its size, an elephant can move almost silently, and in dim light, where it is aided by its camouflage coloring, the animal can seem to appear or disappear quite suddenly.

All elephants have five toes. The African plains elephant has four toenails visible on the front feet and three on the hind feet. The African forest elephant and the Asian elephant have five toenails in front and four in back. In the wild, the toenails wear down with use. At Marine World Africa USA, trainers regularly trim the elephants' toenails to keep them smooth and neat.

Within minutes of its birth, a baby elephant is able to stand up and walk. Instinctively, it positions itself underneath its mother's large body where it is safe from danger. In Africa, predators of young elephants include lions, hyenas, and wild dogs. In Asia, the elephant's predators are mainly tigers.

By the time a young elephant is two days old, it can follow its mother as she moves with the herd. In the wild, elephants move constantly in search of food and water and may walk 10 to 15 miles (16.1 to 24.2 kilometers) each day. Usually elephants walk at speeds of 4 to 5 miles (6.5 to 8.1 kilometers) per hour, although they can run as fast as 24 miles (38.7 kilometers) an hour for a short time.

A wild elephant spends as much as sixteen hours a day eating and looking for food. It needs to eat between 300 and 500 pounds (136.4–227.3 kilograms) of food each day. Its stomach is huge and can hold up to 500 pounds (227.3 kilograms) of food at one time.

Elephants are vegetarians and in the wild they eat a varied diet that includes leaves, grass, fruit, and bark. When a youngster is three or four months old, it begins to eat grass and other plant foods. The young elephant usually stops nursing by the time it is two.

One of the most serious problems for wild elephants today is the difficulty of satisfying their enormous appetites. When feeding, elephants sometimes either strip the bark off trees or knock them over. In the past, when elephants were able to roam freely over vast areas, the trees had time to regrow while the animals fed elsewhere. Now, when elephants are confined to a limited space, they often destroy their food supply faster than it can recover.

Another problem occurs as land becomes developed for agriculture near the parks and preserves where wild elephants live. As food within the preserves becomes scarce, the elephants sometimes eat farmers' crops and so become costly pests. Elephants need a lot of space to live. When room is limited, wildlife managers sometimes have to kill some elephants in order to make sure that there will be enough food for the rest.

The elephants in animal parks and zoos eat about 100 pounds (45.5 kilograms) of hay a day plus a variety of other foods. They eat less than wild animals because they are less active. Also, their foods are more nutritious, so they do not require as much to get the nutrients they need.

At Marine World Africa USA, the elephants are fed most of their food in the barn area where they stay at night. At a special "elephant banquet," however, visitors can watch the elephants eat an assortment of bread, fruit, and vegetables. Mailika is particularly fond of the special San Francisco sourdough bread that she eats a loaf at a time.

The huge molar teeth of an African elephant's lower jaw.

One reason that elephants need to eat so much is that they are not able to digest their food very well. The small and large intestines, where most digestion takes place, are 70 and 40 feet (21.3–12.2 meters) long, respectively. Despite the large size of the intestines, only about 44 percent of the nutrients are extracted as food passes through them.

Another reason that the elephant's food is poorly digested is that the elephants do not chew it very thoroughly. An elephant has only four teeth in its mouth. Each of these large molar teeth, two upper and two lower, may be 1 foot (30.4 centimeters) or more long and weigh up to 8 or 9 pounds (3.6 or 4.1 kilograms). Each tooth is constructed of a series of flat,

The teeth are hidden behind fleshy lips and a thick tongue.

vertical plates that appear as stripes on the surface of the tooth. In the teeth of Asian elephants these plates are narrower than those of African elephants and there are more of them. An Asian elephant tooth may have twenty or more plates, whereas an African tooth has no more than ten.

During its lifetime, an elephant uses six sets of teeth. As one set becomes worn with use, a new set grows in and the old teeth break apart and fall out. Each succeeding tooth is larger than the one before it and has more plates. The last set of molars grows in when the elephant is fifty to sixty years old. In the wild, when these teeth become so worn that the elephant can no longer chew its food, the animal dies of starvation.

Elephants also need water to live. A full-grown elephant needs between 30 and 50 gallons (113.6–189.3 liters) of water a day and can drink as much as 22 gallons (83.3 liters) at one time. An elephant drinks by sucking up several gallons (or liters) of water into its trunk and then squirting it directly down its throat. Elephants also sometimes use their trunks to throw water up over their backs.

In the wild, elephants rarely travel far from water holes or streams where they can drink. At the animal park, the elephants get water along with their food or from troughs in their enclosure. One of the elephants is trained to squirt water on command, a trick that is sometimes performed in the circus ring.

Elephants also need to have salt in their diet. In the wild, they either drink salty water or eat dry salt from natural salt deposits. At the wildlife park, salt and other vitamins and minerals are part of their daily diet.

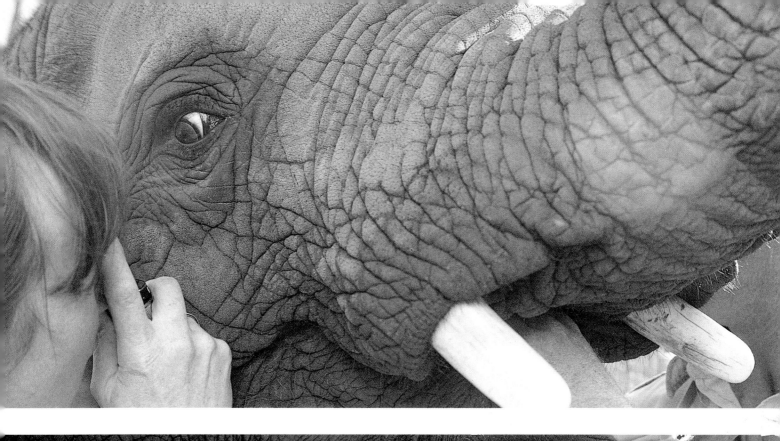

At the wildlife park, the elephants take turns either giving rides or performing in the various demonstrations. When the elephants are not working, they either go into the barn or into one of the large outdoor enclosures.

In one of the enclosures, an old tire makes a good elephant toy and the animals seem to enjoy picking it up and rolling it around. When the weather is warm, Mailika splashes in the water at the edge of the pool. Scientists who study elephants in Africa have observed wild elephants seeming to play, too. Both adults and youngsters sometimes tussle with one another, play tag, or just run about.

The elephants' playful behavior provides exercise and helps to strengthen their muscles and develop coordination.

Because of their tremendous strength, elephants are like living bulldozers. For many centuries, they have been part of the logging industry in Asia. Working singly or in pairs, elephants knock over trees, lift and carry logs, and use a harness to pull lumber through the forest. They can pull up to 2 tons (1.8 metric tons) at one time. Unfortunately, as domestic elephants help people to clear the land of trees, the habitat for wild Asian elephants continues to grow smaller.

At the animal park, elephants exhibit their logging skills in a special demonstration in which they work together to build a wall of logs. And for fun, visitors can test an elephant's pulling strength in a game of tug-of-war. Not surprisingly, the elephant always wins, even with dozens of people tugging on the rope.

Elephants have had a long association with humans. From prehistoric times, people have hunted them for their meat, hides, and tusks. Ancient Egyptians trained African elephants more than 5,000 years ago, and in Asia, elephants have been domesticated for more than 3,000 years. In addition to their use as work animals, elephants have been used for transportation, trained as circus performers, and even revered as religious idols. Ancient warriors sometimes used elephants to carry people and weapons and to frighten the enemy.

Elephants have always been popular zoo and circus animals. The first elephant exhibited in North America was an Asian female that came to New York in 1796. One of the world's most famous elephants was Jumbo, an enormous elephant that lived at the London Zoo for many years before coming to the United States in 1882 to be part of P. T. Barnum's circus. Jumbo died in a train accident in 1885.

Elephants are among the world's most endangered animals. Although they are protected in most places, they continue to be killed illegally for their tusks. Equally threatening is the shrinking of the elephant's natural habitat as the world's human population grows. The challenge for wildlife managers today is to establish a balance between land use for people and for animals like elephants. Elephants are the most visible of a wide variety of species whose homes are rapidly disappearing as people develop wild lands in Africa and Asia for farms, cities, roads, factories, and other uses.

Most of us will never see wild elephants. We can, however, see them in zoos and wildlife parks. Animals such as Mailika help us to learn about elephants and their unique qualities. No other animal has the same combination of size, strength, and intelligence. Elephants have lived on earth for millions of years. Only with a commitment to preserving our natural resources can we make sure that these magnificent animals will continue to have a place in the wild.

INDEX

Photographs are in **boldface**.